W9-BNG-213

REAL TEENS ... REAL ISSUES

DRUG ABUSE

Katie Marsico

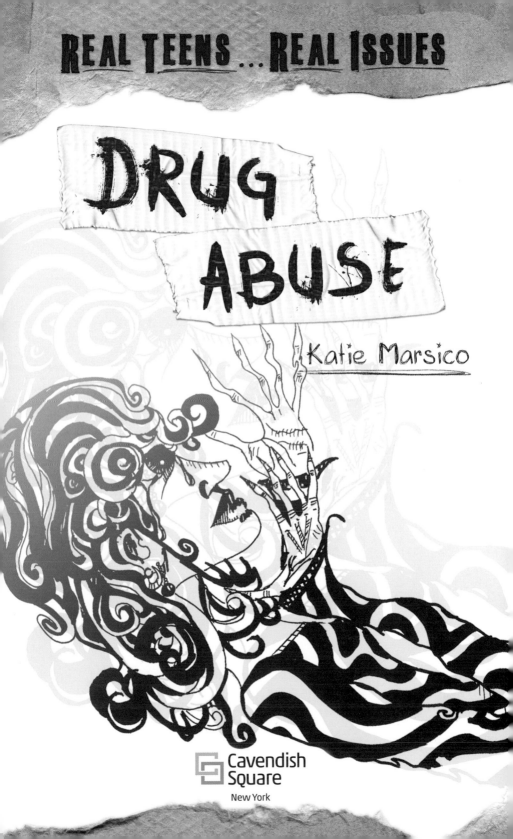

Cavendish
Square

New York

The author would like to dedicate this book to Donna, Josh, Lexie, George Sachs, Judith Hanson, and the wonderful staff at Sobriety High. Finally, she extends her sincere gratitude to her editor, Christine Florie, whose support and guidance in writing this book proved invaluable.

To protect the privacy of sources, only first names are used throughout the book. Any first names that are asterisked (*) indicate the use of a pseudonym.

Published in 2014 by Cavendish Square Publishing, LLC
303 Park Avenue South, Suite 1247, New York, NY 10010

Copyright © 2014 by Cavendish Square Publishing, LLC

First Edition

Website: cavendishsq.com

This publication represents the opinions and views of the author based on his or her personal experience, knowledge, and research. The information in this book serves as a general guide only. The author and publisher have used their best efforts in preparing this book and disclaim liability rising directly or indirectly from the use and application of this book.

CPSIA Compliance Information: Batch #WS13CSQ

All websites were available and accurate when this book was sent to press.

LIBRARY OF CONGRESS CATALOGING-IN-PUBLICATION DATA

Marsico, Katie, 1980–
Drug abuse / Katie Marsico.
p. cm. — (Real teens ... Real issues)
Includes bibliographical references and index.
Summary: "Provides comprehensive information on drug abuse, including first-person interviews, signs and symptoms, physical dangers, recovery, and solutions"—Provided by publisher.
ISBN 978-1-60870-852-9 (hardcover) ISBN 978-1-62712-128-6 (paperback)
ISBN 978-1-60870-858-1 (ebook)
1. Teenagers—Drug use—Juvenile literature. 2. Drug abuse—Prevention—Juvenile literature. 3. Youth—Alcohol use—Juvenile literature. I. Title. II. Series.
HV5824.Y68M365 2013
362.290835—dc23
2011026618

EDITOR: Christine Florie
ART DIRECTOR: Anahid Hamparian   SERIES DESIGNER: Kristen Branch
EXPERT READER: Nicole Bekman, PhD, Project Scientist and Lecturer, Department of Psychology, University of California, San Diego

Photo research by Marybeth Kavanagh

Title page illustration by Corinne Florie

Cover photo by Images.com/Corbis
The photographs in this book are used by permission and through the courtesy of: *Getty Images*: Garry Gay/Photographer's Choice, 4; *Photo Researchers, Inc.*: George Mattei, 8; Ford McCann, 12; Picture Partners, 22; *Superstock*: 11; Lisette Le Bon, 40; age fotostock, 49; *The Image Works*: John Powell/Topham, 21; *Alamy*: Angela Hampton Picture Library, 26; Dennis MacDonald, 30; John Powell Photographer, 32; Steve Hamblin, 36; Steve Skjold, 62; *age fotostock*: MENDIL/BSIP, 43; *PhotoEdit Inc.*: Michael Newman, 51; *Newscom*: Ghislain & Marie David de Lossy Cultura, 54; ZUMA Press, 58. Most subjects in these photos are models.

Printed in the United States of America

CONTENTS

Just
Say
No

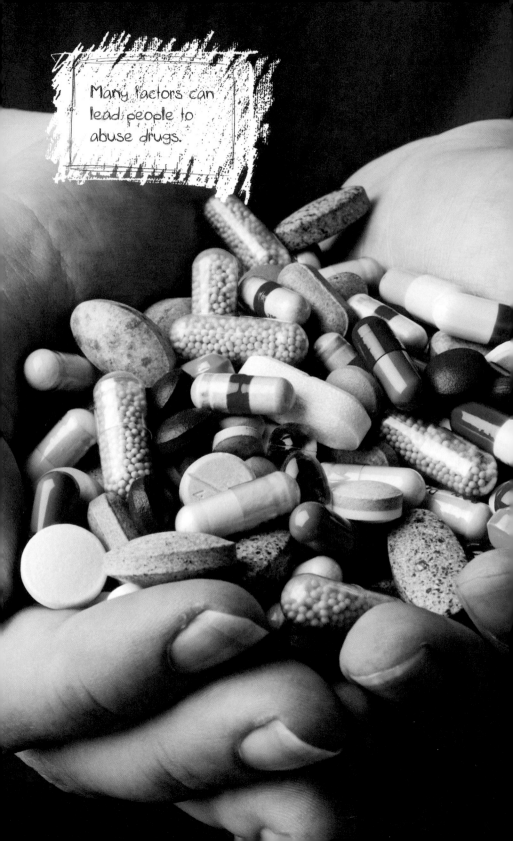

Many factors can lead people to abuse drugs.

ONE

LiVING LiFE TO DO MORE DRUGS

WHILE OTHER HIGH SCHOOL SENIORS split their time between prom committees and college planning, nineteen-year-old Donna is busy working to end a long and destructive relationship with drugs. The Minnesota teenager recalls that she began abusing various substances in eighth grade—not long after her older brother died. In addition to this personal loss, insecurities about her physical appearance and bullying at school shaped much of Donna's **adolescence**.

"All these things took a toll on me," she reflects. "The drugs helped me feel less alone. Gradually, it got to where . . . I simply didn't feel like myself without

5

> "Gradually, it got to where ... I simply didn't feel like myself without having this chemical or that pill in me."
> — Donna

having this chemical or that pill in me." Donna describes experimenting with and abusing a wide range of drugs during this period in her life, including prescription painkillers, marijuana, and cocaine. She also acknowledges that she drank heavily, often to the point of blacking out.

When both her family and faculty members at her school finally demanded that she seek help, she agreed to outpatient counseling for her substance abuse. Donna confesses that, at first, she wasn't happy about being forced into treatment.

STARTLING STAT

A 2010 STUDY REVEALED THAT 8 PERCENT OF TWELFTH GRADERS ADMITTED TO USING THE PAINKILLER HYDRO-CODONE (VICODIN) FOR NONMEDICAL PURPOSES. IN ADDITION, ALMOST 7 PERCENT OF PEOPLE THAT AGE ACKNOWLEDGED THAT THEY ABUSED NONPRESCRIPTION COUGH MEDICATIONS TO GET HIGH.

As time passed, however, her attitude changed. "Initially, I thought I'd do treatment to please my old school," she says. "I had no real desire to be sober. But treatment [gradually] helped me realize that I had a problem I could die from."

Though Donna's struggle with drug abuse—which is also often referred to as substance abuse—has been extremely difficult, describing her new perspective on life is far easier. "Now, I'm doing the recovery program for me—for myself," she emphasizes. "Treatment has taught me how to wake up, and have a different mind-set than I did when I was on drugs. . . . Instead of wanting to get high, I want to learn to be me and shine my own light."

> "Treatment has taught me how to wake up, and have a different mind-set than I did when I was on drugs. . . . Instead of wanting to get high, I want to learn to be me and shine my own light."
> — Donna

UNDERSTANDING DRUG ABUSE

Donna's story is just one example of how drug abuse impacts the lives of millions of American teenagers.

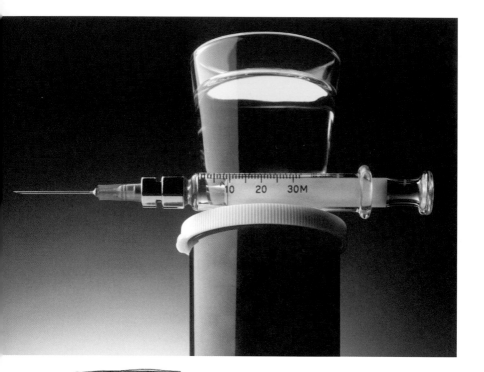

Drug abuse can involve a variety of both legal and illegal substances.

But what exactly does it mean to have this problem? According to the National Institutes of Health (NIH), drug abuse is "the use of illegal drugs or the inappropriate use of legal drugs . . . to produce pleasure, to alleviate stress, or to alter or avoid reality (or all three)."

According to the Experts

George Sachs, PsyD, adds to the definition of drug abuse by explaining the differences among use, abuse, and addiction. Sachs is a licensed clinical psychologist and the founder of the Sachs Center in New York City. This treatment facility addresses a variety of behavioral, developmental, and emotional conditions that frequently affect young people.

"Recreational drug use is typically [defined] as infrequent use of a drug that occurs only in special circumstances and with few to no negative consequences," says Sachs. "On the other hand, abuse is usually thought of in terms of a repeated pattern of drug use that does not stop, despite negative consequences. Abuse interferes with someone's ability to function at home, work, or school. Finally, addiction, or dependence, is described as persistent abuse that often involves a person building up tolerance to a certain drug. Someone who is addicted to drugs generally needs more and more of a particular substance to achieve its desired effect and may experience withdrawal when not using." Sachs emphasizes that recreational drug use can quickly lead to abuse, which, in turn, is capable of transforming into addiction.

DRUG ABUSE

Even though they might disagree on the exact definition of drug abuse, most experts agree that it remains an extremely complicated teen issue. This is partly due to the wide range of methods and substances that people rely on to abuse drugs. For example, the U.S. government has declared certain drugs to be illegal. It is against the law to produce, sell, or distribute these substances, yet that does not stop dealers from pushing them on street corners and in schools. In other cases, abusers use both over-the-counter and prescription medications in a manner that is unsafe or not in keeping with their intended purpose. Finally, some people abuse everyday household products that might not normally be thought of as drugs. In an effort to get high, they inhale the often toxic fumes of chemical-based cleaning solutions, aerosol sprays, paints, and glues.

How do these various substances work to create the physical and mental sensations that make the drugs so appealing to abusers? **Depressants**—one of the three main categories of commonly abused drugs—cause a person's bodily systems to slow down and generally create feelings of sleepiness or relaxation. Alcohol, heroin, and prescription medications

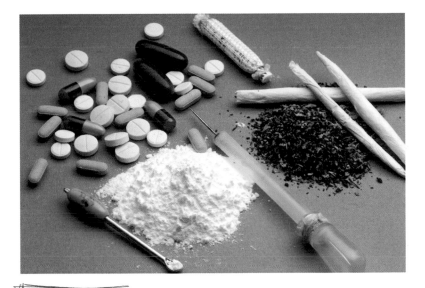

Prescription pills, marijuana, and cocaine are just a few examples of drugs that people abuse.

such as diazepam (Valium) all produce these effects.

Stimulants trigger the exact opposite physical and mental sensations. They speed up the central nervous system and are frequently abused by people seeking increased energy, focus, or productivity. Cocaine and methamphetamines are well-known stimulants, as are medications that physicians sometimes prescribe to treat conditions such as attention deficit/hyperactivity disorder (ADHD).

11

Hallucinogenic drugs, such as magic mushrooms, PCP, LSD, and ecstasy, create altered perceptions of reality. Their ability to uplift or instantly change a person's mood is among the primary reasons why people use **hallucinogens**. Some experts list marijuana as a hallucinogen, but others say it belongs in its own category because it is capable of producing a wide variety of physical and psychological effects. Marijuana is currently the most commonly abused illegal drug in the United States.

Magic mushrooms are a type of hallucinogen.

Living Life to Do More Drugs

Unfortunately, drug abuse—no matter what substance is involved—can have destructive and even deadly consequences. In addition, though not everyone sees an obvious connection between drinking alcohol and doing drugs, the two behaviors are strongly linked. For example, teenagers who drink alcohol are reported to be fifty times more likely to use cocaine than their nondrinking **peers**.

Even when alcohol doesn't play a role in a teen's substance abuse, experimenting with drugs at a party can lead to addiction more quickly and easily than most people imagine. Along the way, abusers often leave a path of broken relationships, damaging physical and mental side effects, and an overwhelming loss of identity behind them.

THE SCOPE OF A SERIOUS ISSUE

A recent study by the U.S. government revealed that roughly 37 percent of high school sophomores and about 42 percent of high school seniors admitted to using **illicit** drugs. It is true that not every person who tries drugs goes on to abuse them. Yet the National Drug Intelligence Center (NDIC) indicates that

13

there is a link between the age at which someone first uses drugs and his or her risk of later developing substance-abuse problems. Researchers with the NDIC determined that people who start using before they turn eighteen are more likely to abuse or become addicted to drugs as adults.

Gender, race, and ethnic background also play a small role in predicting teenage substance abuse. Overall, adolescent boys have slightly higher rates of drug use than adolescent girls. While researchers believe that substance abuse is more common among American Indian teens and less common among Asian Americans, the problem affects every cultural and ethnic group in the United States.

These are not the most startling statistics related to adolescent drug abuse. Accidental drug overdose is listed as the second-leading cause of death among American teenagers. Why are drugs proving to be such a deadly teen issue? Teenagers are at a point in their lives when they are busy developing new relationships, experiencing new situations, and facing new social and academic pressures. For many teens, experimenting with drugs goes hand in hand with this process. Occasional drug use can seem like

STARTLING STAT

DRUG ABUSE PLAYS A SIGNIFICANT ROLE IN TEENAGE
SUICIDE, WHICH IS RANKED AS THE THIRD-LEADING CAUSE
OF DEATH FOR PEOPLE BETWEEN THE AGES OF FIFTEEN
AND TWENTY-FOUR. RESEARCHERS DETERMINED THAT
TEENS WHO HAD RECENTLY USED ILLEGAL DRUGS WERE
THREE TIMES MORE LIKELY TO BE AT RISK OF COMMITTING
SUICIDE THAN THEIR NONUSING PEERS.

---

a harmless indulgence—a typical teen behavior that does not hint at a lifelong habit.

Yet not everyone is fortunate enough to find that this assumption is accurate. In fact, research shows that nearly 1.4 million American teens are struggling with substance abuse. More than two years into recovery, Donna is now grateful to be among the lucky fraction of the group that got help. "At first, I was resentful that I got caught and had to do treatment," she says. "But now I stop and consider how things would be if that hadn't happened. If I hadn't changed my life, I think I might very well be half-dead right now."

TWO

TRIGGERS AND TYPICAL WARNING SIGNS

SEVENTEEN-YEAR-OLD LEXIE REMEM-bers that as a freshman in high school, she was already abusing ecstasy and an antianxiety medication called alprazolam (Xanax). By her sophomore year, the California teen had added cocaine and over-the-counter cough medicine to the list of substances she relied on to get high. It wasn't long before Lexie began experimenting with heroin as well. While abusing these drugs, she also drank heavily—a practice she recalls starting in eighth grade.

STARTLING STAT

RESEARCH SHOWS THAT APPROXIMATELY 75 PERCENT OF FEMALE PATIENTS BEING TREATED FOR SUBSTANCE ABUSE HAVE ALSO EXPERIENCED SOME FORM OF SEXUAL ABUSE.

For Lexie, the root of her problems traces much further back than adolescence. When she was just five years old, her stepfather began sexually abusing her. This behavior traumatized Lexie and, by the time she was a teenager, led her to view drugs as a source of escape and comfort. Her stepfather helped set the stage for her substance abuse in other ways, too. As a methamphetamine addict, he exposed Lexie to drugs and—in what she now concludes was an effort to keep her quiet about his molestation—even bought them for her.

"My stepdad basically facilitated my drug abuse," she explains. "He made me feel like it was something that allowed us to relate to one another. Being sexually molested by him was one of the reasons I started doing drugs, and he also became an opportunity for me to continue doing them."

> "Being sexually molested by [my stepfather] was one of the reasons I started doing drugs, and he also became an opportunity for me to continue doing them."
>
> — Lexie

Eventually, it became clear that Lexie's drinking and drug use were taking an increasingly heavy toll on her health. At one point, she was even hospitalized for blacking out during a party. Her mother ultimately arranged for her to receive treatment at an inpatient facility. Like so many people who abuse drugs, Lexie initially denied her problem and resisted outside support in dealing with it. A year later, however, she has a far different point of view.

Now in outpatient treatment, Lexie has discovered how to open up about her feelings and the day-to-day challenges she faces while working to maintain sobriety. "I [have] learned not to lie about my drug abuse and what caused it," she concludes. "I have found that, in the end, you'll never get away with the lies you tell."

"I [have] learned not to lie about my drug abuse and what caused it. I have found that, in the end, you'll never get away with the lies you tell." — **Lexie**

RAISING THE RISK OF A SERIOUS PROBLEM

What puts people like Lexie at greater risk of suffering from substance abuse? Unsurprisingly, there is no simple answer to this question, just as no two individuals have identical drug problems. What researchers *do* know is that several factors consistently appear to increase a person's risk of abusing drugs.

"Genetics and family history most definitely play a role," explains Judith Hanson, the director of community and family outreach at Sobriety High. This Minnesota charter-school system provides ninth- to twelfth-grade students with a supportive, sober learning atmosphere where they can attend classes and earn their diplomas. Since Sobriety High is a recovery-based program for teenagers who have experienced substance abuse, Hanson is well aware of the many

"Studies have shown that teenagers are four times more likely to abuse drugs if one of their parents does. They are nine times more likely to suffer from substance abuse if both parents do."
— Judith Hanson

risk factors involved in that teen issue. "Studies have shown that teenagers are four times more likely to abuse drugs if one of their parents does," she continues. "They are nine times more likely to suffer from substance abuse if both parents do."

Apart from genetics, low self-esteem and the stress of not fitting in to mainstream social groups also increase a person's likelihood of abusing drugs. In addition, several comorbid conditions—including eating disorders, depression, and anxiety—place people at a higher risk of having a drug problem. Experts believe that

STARTLING STAT

RECENT STUDIES SUGGEST THAT 30 PERCENT OF TEENS WHO SUFFER FROM DEPRESSION EVENTUALLY STRUGGLE WITH SUBSTANCE ABUSE AS WELL.

Certain experts believe that low self-esteem can sometimes set the stage for drug abuse to occur.

bullying, sexual molestation, and any form of physical or verbal abuse have a similar effect.

COMMON SYMPTOMS OF SUBSTANCE ABUSE

Drug abuse is not always easy to spot, especially because different substances produce different side effects. For example, depressants typically cause increased sleepiness, whereas stimulants may trigger the people who use them to have abnormally high energy levels. Yet medical experts say that individuals who abuse drugs frequently share certain physical, emotional, and social characteristics.

Many drug abusers complain of fatigue and experience disrupted sleep patterns. Their eyes may appear red, glazed, or bloodshot, and their pupils might seem either larger or smaller than usual. People who are abusing drugs may also display sudden changes in appetite and weight. In addition, they are sometimes

One possible sign of drug abuse is increased or unusual fatigue.

less attentive to their physical appearance and may smell of odors that are associated with smoking drugs. Others demonstrate slurred speech or uncoordinated movements, which are especially common side effects of abusing depressants.

These physical clues aren't the only hints that someone is developing a drug problem. Sudden mood or personality changes also indicate potential substance abuse. People who abuse drugs frequently display poor judgment and irresponsible behavior. They may seem more irritable than usual and, in some cases, almost eager to break rules or to pick fights with others.

Another warning sign that a person is abusing drugs is a sudden lack of interest in activities or relationships that once gave that individual a sense of pride or pleasure. Someone might shy away from social and family events that he or she previously enjoyed participating in. The person might even seem to abandon long-term relationships for new friends who are known to regularly use or have access to drugs.

"Any major changes in the type of people that teenagers normally hang out with can be a big red flag

"Any major changes in the type of people that teenagers normally hang out with can be a big red flag that drug abuse is occurring. The same is true when it comes to an unexplained shift in grades."
— Judith Hanson

that drug abuse is occurring," emphasizes Hanson. "The same is true when it comes to an unexplained shift in grades." People who are struggling with substance abuse also tend to leave other clues in the classroom. They may start showing up late to school or begin having more unexcused absences or discipline problems. Though their grades suddenly slip, they typically display little concern about their negative academic performance.

While many people attempt to hide their drug abuse, some unintentionally reveal the truth in day-to-day conversation. A person's friends may notice that he or she talks about getting high all the time or obsesses over the next opportunity to use a particular substance. Other obvious clues that peers or family members might pick up on include track marks or needle wounds on the person's skin. They may also observe the presence of drug paraphernalia on

Avoid Assumptions!

If parents and peers suspect that someone they care about is abusing drugs, Lexie advises them to take immediate action. She strongly warns against making the potentially fatal assumption that the person will be able to fix his or her problem independently.

"If you suspect or know that a teenager has a drug problem, try to get them help right away," she urges. "Do not put it off! Don't create or accept excuses for the person that justify the situation or that make it seem less important than it really is."

Problems at school can hint at a possible drug problem.

someone's clothes or among his or her personal belongings. Finally, friends and family can safely assume that a person who has blacked out, overdosed, or required emergency medical treatment due to drug use most likely has a serious problem.

26

THREE

THE HARM IN GETTING HIGH

EIGHTEEN-YEAR-OLD JOSH CLEARLY recalls the time he woke up wondering why he had bruises and scratches all over his face. In the week leading up to his mysterious injuries, the Minnesota teen had been drinking and using drugs almost nonstop. Eventually, Josh remembered that he had stumbled home from a friend's house the night before—falling and hitting the pavement several times along the way.

Yet cuts and bruises were only a few of the side effects he experienced during half a decade of substance abuse. Before his drug problem started negatively impacting his health, he had an athletic build

> **"I don't think people realize that marijuana can be an incredibly harmful drug. It kills your lungs *and* your brain cells." —Josh**

that reflected years of participating in such sports as football, wrestling, hockey, and baseball. As his abuse worsened, though, Josh shed about 50 pounds. Smoking cigarettes and marijuana also took a significant toll on his body. "I was coughing left and right," Josh notes. "I don't think people realize that marijuana can be an incredibly harmful drug. It kills your lungs *and* your brain cells."

Josh is quick to emphasize that substance abuse seriously impacted far more than his body. "My drive to do anything—to accomplish anything—

STARTLING STAT

MEDICAL EXPERTS HAVE DETERMINED THAT MARIJUANA SMOKE CONTAINS MORE THAN FOUR HUNDRED CHEMICALS AND 50 TO 70 PERCENT MORE CANCER-CAUSING TOXINS THAN CIGARETTE SMOKE.

"If I had continued on the path I was on . . . I would most likely be lying in a ditch somewhere. Substance abuse is truly a disease that takes over everything." — Josh

was virtually gone," he reflects. "As far as my sports performance, it was obvious I started slacking when it came to the workouts and physical conditioning that coaches pay close attention to. If you have effort, you have game . . . and I didn't have effort." By his senior year, this shift in attitude and performance cost him several opportunities to advance within his high school's athletic program.

Fortunately, Josh completed treatment and has been sober since the summer of 2010. No matter how much time passes, though, he doubts that he will ever forget how drugs jeopardized his physical and emotional health. "If I had continued on the path I was on, I don't know if I'd be alive," he says. "I would most likely be lying in a ditch somewhere. Substance abuse is truly a disease that takes over everything."

29

Drug abuse can negatively affect athletic performance.

THE HARM IN GETTING HIGH

BRUTAL EFFECTS ON THE BODY

Being young doesn't guarantee that a person will be spared the physical dangers that go hand in hand with substance abuse. In fact, experts believe that teenagers who abuse drugs face potentially greater health risks *because* of their age. "Parts of the human body aren't even fully developed until much later in life," explains Judith Hanson. "By doing drugs, you're essentially taking in chemicals that could have a serious impact on the way your body should normally grow and change throughout adolescence."

Substance abuse has a wide range of physical effects that often depend on what specific drug is involved, as well as how much of it is being used. Other factors include how long a person has been abusing drugs and how frequently drugs are taken.

Common physical reactions to drugs include dangerous swings in heart rate, body temperature,

> **"By doing drugs, you're essentially taking in chemicals that could have a serious impact on the way your body should normally grow and change through-out adolescence."**
> **— Judith Hanson**

blood pressure, and breathing rate. Weight changes, sweating, dehydration, dizziness, trembling, head-aches, sleep disruption, and vision problems are also common. Abusers often demonstrate slurred speech or complain of stomach upset and skin irritation as well. In extreme cases, drug abuse can trigger **seizures**, loss of consciousness, and brain damage.

Loss of consciousness can be one physical result of drug abuse.

In many situations, it is not just the drugs alone but the methods in which they are taken that lead to various health problems. For example, abusing marijuana, crack, or other substances that people generally smoke or inhale is harmful to the nose, mouth, throat, and lungs. Like Josh, individuals who abuse these drugs may experience a constant cough, unusual wheezing, and increased respiratory illnesses. Equally terrifying is the havoc that drugs often wreak on a person's mind.

HOW DRUGS HARM THE HUMAN MIND

Teenagers aren't always aware of the devastating impact that substance abuse has on their young bodies—or the heavy toll it takes on their mental and emotional health. Since drugs directly affect people's brains and

STARTLING STAT

RESEARCH SHOWS THAT ABOUT 25 PERCENT OF HIV/AIDS CASES IN THE UNITED STATES ARE THE RESULT OF INTRAVENOUS DRUG USERS SHARING NEEDLES.

nervous systems, they inevitably influence feelings, impulses, and reactions as well.

According to researchers with a health-resource organization called Helpguide, "All abused substances share one thing in common: they hijack the brain's normal 'reward' pathways and alter the areas of the brain [that are] responsible for self-control, judgment, emotional regulation, motivation, memory, and learning." Such side effects frequently set the stage for disaster. Substance abuse raises the risk that someone will have unprotected sex, drive under the influence of drugs, or act in other ways that either jeopardize safety or break the law.

In addition, substance abuse can cause hallucinations, paranoia, confusion, and intense mood swings. Depending on the drug being used, abusers tend to show signs of aggression, anxiety, or depression as

"All abused substances ... hijack the brain's 'reward' pathways and alter the areas of the brain [that are] responsible for self-control, judgement, ... and learning." — **Helpguide**

A Significant Student Issue

The physical and mental effects of living with substance abuse inevitably shape how teenagers perform in both the classroom and extracurricular activities. "My grades definitely started slipping as my substance abuse worsened," says Josh. "It's not too surprising, though. You can't get much homework done when you're high as a kite."

For Josh a bigger challenge than maintaining focus was finding the desire and determination to succeed—or even to barely scrape by—academically. "It wasn't so much about not being able to concentrate to get the work accomplished," he observes. "It was more about me having zero motivation to do anything."

Drugs can cause hallucinations, and extreme confusion, and paranoia.

their high wears off. After a while, some people feel like they have no control over what is basically an emotional roller-coaster ride. As a result, many abusers are more likely to develop serious depression and stress, which can end in a tragic outcome, such as suicide.

FOUR

AN ISSUE THAT IMPACTS RELATIONSHIPS

NINETEEN-YEAR-OLD DONNA IS PAIN-
fully aware of how her drug problem has affected the
people who love and care
about her. The Minnesota
teen acknowledges that as
she began abusing drugs,
her relationship with her
mother and father gradually
transformed into a vicious
cycle of anger, denial, and
misunderstanding. "I was a
monster to my family," she
recalls. "Screaming, breaking

> "I was a monster to
> my family—screaming,
> breaking things, throw-
> ing things. Deep down,
> I never wanted to be a
> disappointment to my
> parents, but I guess I
> really was." — **Donna**

things, throwing things. Deep down, I never wanted to be a disappointment to my parents, but I guess I really was."

Donna's relationship with her family was strained as a result of her drug abuse, and her connections with her peers were not much better. "I didn't really have any friends when I was using," she notes. "Drugs allowed me to forget that I felt lonely." After undergoing treatment, Donna is better able to appreciate and build healthy connections with other people. Throughout this process she has also been gaining a painful understanding of how drug abuse devastates relationships—and makes them complicated to repair.

> "Drugs allowed me to forget that I felt lonely." — Donna

STARTLING STAT

THE NATIONAL SURVEY ON DRUG USE AND HEALTH (NSDUH) SHOWED THAT TEENS WHO HAD RECENTLY USED AN ILLICIT DRUG WERE NEARLY TWICE AS LIKELY TO DISPLAY VIOLENT BEHAVIOR THAN THEIR NONUSING PEERS.

SHORT-CIRCUITING
SOCIAL DEVELOPMENT

According to Judith Hanson, drugs alter the way people process feelings and emotions. In many cases, the end result is what she describes as a "short-circuiting" of teenagers' ability to explore and create healthy relationships. "The teen years are a time when kids are learning social skills, discovering who they are, and gradually building confidence based on that knowledge," she notes. "When they put a chemical in them that blocks out or transforms their natural feelings, teenagers are essentially retreating from valuable life experiences."

Since drugs impact a person's emotions and behavior, they affect not only abusers but also the people around them. Substance abuse commonly leads to increased anxiety, aggression, and depression, which inevitably shape users' relationships with friends and family members. Both getting high and the physical and psychological "crash" that follows often trigger dramatic mood swings and disruptive, violent outbursts.

For parents and friends who are unaware of a person's drug abuse, dealing with these unpredictable

Drug abuse often seriously strains a person's relationship with his or her parents.

emotions can be confusing and hurtful. In addition, the dishonesty and mistrust that frequently go hand in hand with drug problems further complicate the abuser's personal relationships. Drug abusers often lie to conceal their drug use from family members or peers whom they know would disapprove. Some also break curfew, miss work or school, steal from parents

STARTLING STAT

EXPERTS SAY THAT ALMOST 46 PERCENT OF TEENS WHO
ABUSE ONE MAIN DRUG DEMONSTRATE VIOLENT BEHAV-
IOR. THAT RATE CLIMBS TO NEARLY 62 PERCENT FOR
TEENAGERS WHO HAVE A DRUG PROBLEM INVOLVING
THREE OR MORE SUBSTANCES.

and friends, or behave in other ways that cause them to be labeled as unreliable and untrustworthy.

As abusers fall deeper into a cycle of substance abuse, several start to withdraw from what were once meaningful relationships. Instead of turning to people who previously provided love and support, they begin spending more time with other users or anyone who can offer them access to drugs. In the end, however, these new relationships rarely prove healthy, stable, or helpful in overcoming substance abuse.

TURNING POINTS
AND TANGLED EMOTIONS

If they are lucky, abusers ultimately reach a turning point in their battle with drugs. Regardless of whether

> "When teens begin abusing drugs, their main relationship is with drugs. Anything or anyone who gets in the way of that relationship is a potential threat."
> — George Sachs

people seek help on their own or someone forces them to pursue it, they are ideally taking the first steps on a path to recovery. Yet this does not automatically heal all of the personal relationships that have been strained or damaged by their drug abuse. In fact, sometimes things get worse before they get better. "When teens begin abusing drugs, their main relationship is with drugs," explains George Sachs. "Anything or anyone who gets in the way of that relationship is a potential threat."

Some abusers ultimately grasp that treatment is an opportunity to regain control of their lives. Nevertheless, it is difficult to predict how much time will pass and how much damage their problem will cause before they reach this point. Meanwhile, their friends and family members still must face their own fears and emotions.

Like abusers themselves, the people around them may experience denial, too. This reaction is not

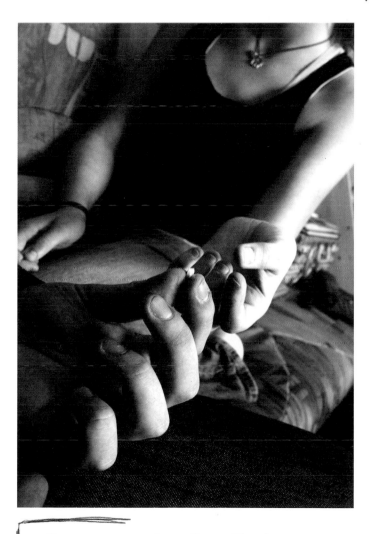

For someone struggling with abuse or addiction, drugs can become more important than personal relationships.

Another Person's Point of View

Like Donna's friends and family members, many people who watch someone they care about struggle with drug abuse can relate to the pain and frustration that go hand in hand with that experience. As the grandmother of seventeen-year-old Lexie (profiled in Chapter Two), Gail describes living through a roller-coaster ride of emotions as her granddaughter battled drugs.

"It was an awful few years," she recalls. "I watched Lexie spiraling downward and tried over and over to ease her fall. I spent every hour of every day worried sick about her. The depth of [my] fear and pain was almost indescribable. It was hard to focus on much else." Since Lexie began treatment and recovery, however, Gail insists that they are gradually repairing and re-building their relationship.

"We talk and laugh," she explains. "When Lexie struggles, we work together to get her back on track quickly. She is learning how to function normally again. . . . For the first time ever, I really feel hopeful that at the end of the day she will overcome her pain and obstacles and have a good life. I am blessed to have her!"

unusual for parents, siblings, and peers who suspect that they have somehow caused a person's problem with drugs. Denying the severity of someone's drug abuse is also a common response to frustration about not having recognized or dealt with it sooner.

Ultimately, friends, family members, and the abusers they care about are often uncertain about the future. Most quickly realize that starting treatment is not a fast, easy solution to repairing damaged relationships. Yet getting help *does* remind people that they have their entire lives ahead of them—and that they can choose a future that is not controlled by drugs.

FIVE

GETTING CLEAN AND STAYING SOBER

EIGHTEEN-YEAR-OLD JOSH ADMITS that he initially didn't take treatment for his drug problem seriously. While no one forced the Minnesota teen to enter the first outpatient program he participated in, he acknowledges that he definitely didn't make the most of the experience.

"After I left treatment, I **relapsed**," he says. "I kept doing drugs throughout the remainder of the year. It was still really hard for me to grasp that I couldn't even occasionally use. I developed a pattern of relapsing, getting clean, and then relapsing again."

Josh explains that one of the breakthrough moments that finally helped him make significant

> "It was still really hard for me to grasp that I couldn't even occasionally use. I developed a pattern of relapsing, getting clean, and then relapsing again." — **Josh**

progress occurred in the summer of 2010. "I was at work, and I kept hearing this thumping noise against the window," he recollects. "I went over to check it out and saw this little yellow bird that kept flying into the glass. I'd seen birds crash into windows before, but this one did it over and over—like seven or eight times. That was my big 'aha' moment. I suddenly told myself, 'Quit making the same mistake twice!'"

Josh has been sober since June 2010. He decided to enroll in Sobriety High in January 2011 so that

STARTLING STAT

RESEARCH INDICATES THAT 40 TO 60 PERCENT OF PATIENTS WHO RECEIVE TREATMENT FOR SUBSTANCE ABUSE EVENTUALLY EXPERIENCE A RELAPSE.

he could earn his high school diploma alongside peers, teachers, and counselors who are committed to supporting his recovery. "I feel like everything's looking up for me," he concludes. "I'm working with a great sponsor that I met during treatment, and I now know what it means to have hope. Yet I also understand that I need to deal with my life twenty-four hours at a time."

> "I feel like everything's looking up for me . . . and I now know what it means to have hope. Yet I also understand that I need to deal with my life twenty-four hours at a time."
> — Josh

ACCEPTING HELP AND GRADUALLY HEALING

Overcoming drug abuse is rarely easy, but people have far more options and opportunities for rehabilitation—treatment and recovery—than they did several decades ago. The type of programming someone participates in depends on many factors, including the nature and severity of the drug abuse. Sometimes a person tries out one or more treatment approaches before realizing that an alternative facility or recovery plan would be a better fit.

Regardless of what program abusers ultimately rely upon to address their problems, several find that their earliest efforts at getting better involve detoxification. Commonly referred to as detox, this process can last days, weeks, or as long as it takes to cleanse the body of whatever drugs they have been using. For people battling especially severe substance abuse, it is a stage of recovery that frequently involves painful

Detoxification can be a physically and emotionally draining process.

and terrifying withdrawal symptoms. This is one of the reasons why most drug-abuse experts recommend that patients detox under the supervision and care of medical professionals.

After abusers get clean, they generally continue their treatment in counseling. This portion of recovery often includes psychotherapy, or talk therapy, with a trained therapist, counselor, psychologist, or psychiatrist. During psychotherapy, patients explore why they began using drugs, as well as how substance abuse has impacted their physical and emotional health and their personal relationships.

There are many different kinds of psychotherapy, and therapists usually recommend one or more types based on someone's specific needs and situation. For instance, many substance-abuse treatment programs offer cognitive behavioral therapy. People who participate in this type of counseling work with therapists to identify any comorbid conditions or negative behaviors or ideas that are contributing to their drug problem. Patients then develop plans to make positive changes in their attitudes and day-to-day choices and actions. Most do this with the long-term goal of enjoying a drug-free future.

In addition to cognitive behavioral therapy, many people receiving treatment for substance abuse are involved in group and family counseling. During group therapy, patients share their experiences and exchange support with other people facing similar issues. In family therapy, abusers and their friends and relatives discuss the best ways to repair relationships that have been affected by drugs.

Family counseling can benefit both former drug abusers and the people who care about them.

DRUG ABUSE

TREATMENT OPTIONS
AND RECOVERY EFFORTS

How do people working to overcome a drug problem decide between inpatient and outpatient treatment? Inpatient, or residential, programs tend to be better for people struggling with severe or long-term substance abuse. This also may be the best option for people who have suffered an overdose or whose behavior threatens their own safety or the safety of others. Trained staff can closely monitor patients who fit this description to ensure that they remain as healthy and stable as possible throughout treatment. Most inpatient programs last an average of thirty days, though some are shorter or longer. Many people start off doing an inpatient program and eventually switch to an outpatient program that lasts anywhere from two months to one year.

Since old habits die hard, drug-abuse experts recommend that people develop a detailed sobriety plan with their friends, family members, and any medical professionals and counselors overseeing their recovery. Long-term strategies for staying clean frequently include attending aftercare counseling on a regular basis, joining community or school support

Reflections and Realizations

As someone who's spent the past four years in recovery, twenty-six-year-old Tyler has experienced his share of ups and downs since initially getting high at age twelve. "After I tried heroin . . . everything I loved and cared about fell to the wayside," he explains. "I was basically hopeless."

Tyler has overdosed on multiple occasions and—after starting treatment and recovery in 2007—has periodically relapsed. Yet he also takes pride in having remained sober since August 2008 by attending support meetings and spending time with other recovering addicts who provide him with encouragement. In turn, he is eager to offer help to teens who are struggling with substance abuse.

"I guess I would tell a teenager in recovery to do it for no one but themselves," Tyler emphasizes. "Do it for you, so you can achieve things in life. So that you don't wake up one day and find that years have gone by, and there's nothing you can do about it. Finally, know that life is not over when you stop getting high. In fact, it's just beginning."

Support groups can provide people in recovery with the tools they need for long-term sobriety.

STARTLING STAT

Experts estimate that only 10 percent of teens struggling with substance abuse receive treatment.

groups, and following a twelve-step program. This type of programming typically features a dozen principles or traditions that people are advised to reflect on and put into action in their lives. The steps are designed to help people achieve physical, mental, emotional, and sometimes spiritual recovery.

Many individuals find that they are more likely to accomplish this goal if they actively communicate with a sponsor. Sponsors are basically mentors who commit to aiding someone through the recovery process. Since most sponsors have also struggled with drugs, they understand what patients are experiencing and can offer practical advice on how to stay clean. Their mission—like that of the medical professionals, counselors, family members, and friends who support people battling substance abuse—is to help people look ahead toward a drug-free future.

SIX

TEENS' IDEAS ON TACKLING DRUG ABUSE

D**RUG ABUSE IS NOTHING NEW TO** society, yet it remains a large-scale problem that people across the globe are struggling to solve. Many people have developed various ideas and opinions about what strategies might prove successful in attacking this teen issue at its roots.

"High school is a pretty tough place for kids to stay sober," observes seventeen-year-old Lexie of California. "That's why it would make a difference if schools created more support groups for students who are affected by substance abuse. It's important for teens to feel like they can talk about this issue and get help for it in a safe environment."

> "[I]t would make a difference if schools created more support groups for students who are affected by substance abuse. It's important for teens to feel like they can talk about this issue and get help for it in a safe environment." — **Lexie**

George Sachs agrees and adds that parents and school officials need to take things a step beyond simply telling the public that drugs can be deadly. "The most common preventive approach to teen drug abuse is promoting education and awareness," he says. "There are already a number of programs in schools and communities that educate people about the dangers of drug abuse, but they're only part of

STARTLING STAT

RESEARCH REVEALS THAT MORE THAN 60 PERCENT OF TEENAGERS REPORTED PEOPLE SELLING, USING, OR STORING DRUGS AT THEIR SCHOOLS.

Law enforcement officers try to help educate the public about the dangers of drug abuse and how to seek help for this problem.

the equation.... Increasing counseling opportunities and normalizing help-seeking behaviors would also be effective solutions."

USING REALITY TO RESHAPE SOCIAL ATTITUDES

Nineteen-year-old Donna of Minnesota shares Lexie's and Sachs's opinions. Yet she also believes that many Americans continue to struggle with drug problems as a result of society's attitudes toward substance abuse. Donna specifically feels that not everyone understands or accepts the realities of this issue. "I think more people need to be aware that teens who are dealing with drug and alcohol abuse actually do have legitimate problems," she remarks. "Once you're abusing drugs, you can't just stop because you feel like it."

> "I think more people need to be aware that teens who are dealing with drug and alcohol abuse actually do have legitimate problems. Once you're abusing drugs, you can't just stop because you feel like it." — **Donna**

According to Judith Hanson, part of the responsibility of getting real about teens' drug problems lies with parents. "Adults need to be role models," she explains. "How they act and what they say can make substance abuse seem like an accepted norm. That gives many kids a sense of entitlement to drink or do drugs because they think those behaviors are okay. For this reason, parents absolutely have to avoid giving mixed messages about drugs."

STARTLING STAT

ACCORDING TO A RECENT STUDY, 74 PERCENT OF TEENS
SAY THEIR PARENTS WOULD BE THE FIRST PEOPLE THEY'D
APPROACH FOR ADVICE ON MATTERS RELATED TO ALCOHOL
AND DRUGS.

USING EXPERIENCE TO OFFER SUPPORT

Along with Donna and Lexie, eighteen-year-old Josh realizes that he doesn't necessarily have an easy road ahead of him. Yet he is now able to perceive the good that has come from these challenges. "I went through tough times like everyone else has," the Minnesota teen reflects. "But I wouldn't change a single thing about what I've been through. What I've dealt with and how I've dealt with it have made me the person I am today."

Josh also believes that he and recovering abusers like him can offer their help and support when people decide they're ready to deal with their problems. That is why he shares his story when he travels to various schools to speak as an ambassador for Sobriety High. "The wonderful thing about talking to other

"The wonderful thing about talking to other teenagers about what I've been through is that we all understand each other. It's important to make kids who are dealing with or recovering from substance abuse aware that they are not alone." — **Josh**

Show Your Support!

Americans recognize September as Recovery Month and October as Drug Abuse Prevention Month. Use this time to talk to school officials or community leaders about hanging posters or distributing flyers that list drug-abuse warning signs, statistics, and treatment options. Alternatively, think about starting your own local support group for teens who are dealing with substance abuse.

teenagers about what I've been through is that we all understand each other," says Josh. "It's important to make kids who are dealing with or recovering from substance abuse aware that they are not alone."

Josh, Lexie, Donna, and countless friends, family members, and treatment and recovery workers are determined to accomplish this goal—and to help young people overcome this teen issue.

People of all ages and backgrounds can do their part to raise awareness about drug abuse and to offer support to those who are struggling with it.

Status Update on Teen Sources

As of late 2011 . . .

DONNA reports preparing to celebrate three years of sobriety on October 16, 2011. Once she finishes high school, she hopes to study to become an art teacher.

LEXIE says she is planning on graduating from high school in April 2012. After that, she intends to attend a community college where she can take courses in general education and communication.

JOSH indicates that he is enrolled in college and continues to share his insights, experiences, and support with other young people dealing with drug abuse.

Notes

CHAPTER 1

p. 5, "All these things took a toll . . .": Donna. Personal interview. 16 February 2011.

p. 6, "A 2010 study revealed that . . .": statistical data on the percentage of twelfth-grade students who admit to using both prescription and nonprescription drugs to get high, "NIDA InfoFacts: High School and Youth Trends," the National Institute on Drug Abuse (NIDA), (specific date last updated not available) August 2010, www.drugabuse.gov/infofacts/hsyouthtrends.html.

p. 7, "Initially, I thought I'd do . . .": Donna. Personal interview. 16 February 2011.

p. 7, "Now, I'm doing the recovery . . .": Donna. Personal interview. 16 February 2011.

p. 8, "the use of illegal . . .": verbiage of definition of drug abuse, "The Essence of Drug Addiction," the National Institutes of Health (NIH), (specific date last updated not available) 2007, www.ncbi.nlm.nih.gov/books/NBK20368.

p. 9, "Recreational drug use is . . .": Sachs, George. Personal interview. 27 February 2011.

p. 13, "For example, teenagers who . . .": statistical data on the likelihood that teenagers who drink alcohol will also abuse cocaine, "Statistics on Alcohol Abuse," Learn-About-Alcoholism.com, (specific date last updated not available), www.learn-about-alcoholism.com/statistics-on-alcohol-abuse.html.

p. 13, "A recent study by the . . .": statistical data on the percentage of high school sophomores and seniors who have admitted to using illicit drugs, "NIDA InfoFacts: High School and Youth Trends," NIDA, (specific date last updated not available) August 2010, www.drugabuse.gov/infofacts/hsyouthtrends.html.

p. 15, "Drug abuse plays . . .": statistical data on where suicide ranks as a cause of death for fifteen- to twenty-four-year-olds, "Facts and Figures," the America Foundation for Suicide Prevention (AFSP), (specific date last updated not available) 2011, www.afsp.org/index.cfm?fuseaction=home. viewpage&page_id=050fea9f-b064-4092-b1135c3a70de1fda.

p. 15, "Researchers determined that teens who . . .": statistical data on the suicide risk for teens who smoke marijuana, "Marijuana and Teens," the San Dieguito Alliance for Drug Free Youth, (specific date last updated not available), www.sandieguitoalliance.org/marijuanaandteens.html.

p. 15, "In fact, research shows . . .": statistical data on the number of U.S. teens struggling with drug abuse, "Treating Adolescents with Addiction," the Ohio Association of County Behavioral Health Authorities (OACBHA), (specific date last updated not available), 2011, www.oacbha.org/wp-content/uploads/2011/Session%20J%20-%20Treating%20Adolescents%20with%20Addiction.pdf.

p. 15, "At first, I was . . .": Donna. Personal interview. 16 February 2011.

DRUG ABUSE

CHAPTER 2

p. 17, "Research indicates that approximately . . .": statistical data on the percentage of female drug abusers who have also experienced physical or sexual abuse, "Drug Treatment for Women," Drug and Alcohol Detoxification Centers, (specific date last updated not available), www.drugalcoholdetoxcenters.com/aarticles-drug-treatment-for-women.html.

p. 17, "My stepdad basically facilitated . . .": Lexie. Personal interview. 1 July 2010.

p. 19, "I [have] learned not to . . .": Lexie. Personal interview. 1 July 2010.

p. 19, "Genetics and family history . . .": Hanson, Judith. Personal interview. 1 March 2011.

pp. 19-20, "Studies have shown that . . .": Hanson, Judith. Personal interview. 1 March 2011.

p. 20, "Recent studies suggest that . . .": statistical data on the percentage of depressed teenagers who develop problems with substance abuse, "Teenage Depression Statistics," Teen Depression, (specific date last updated not available), www.teendepression.org/stats/teenage-depression-statistics.

pp. 23-24, "Any major changes in . . .": Hanson, Judith. Personal interview. 1 March 2011.

p. 25, "If you suspect or know . . .": Lexie. Personal interview. 2 March 2011.

CHAPTER 3

p. 28, "I was coughing left and . . .": Josh. Personal interview. 1 March 2011.

NOTES

p. 28, "Medical experts have determined . . .": statistical data on the chemical makeup of marijuana, "Fiction: Marijuana Is Harmless," Just Think Twice, (specific date last updated not available), www.justthinktwice.com/factsfiction/fiction_marijuana_is_harmless.html.

pp. 28–29, "My drive to do anything . . .": Josh. Personal interview. 1 March 2011.

p. 29, "If I had continued on . . .": Josh. Personal interview. 3 March 2011.

p. 31, "Parts of the human body . . .": Hanson, Judith. Personal interview. 1 March 2011.

p. 33, "Research shows that about . . .": statistical data linking HIV/AIDS cases in the United States to intravenous drug use, "NIDA InfoFacts: Drug Abuse and the Link to HIV/AIDS and Other Infectious Diseases," NIDA, (specific date last updated not available) July 2011, www.nida.nih.gov/Infofacts/drugabuse.html.

p. 34, "All abused substances share . . .": verbiage describing characteristics of abused substances, "Drug Abuse and Addiction," Helpguide, (specific date last updated not available) November 2010, www.helpguide.org/mental/drug_substance_abuse_addiction_signs_effects_treatment.htm.

p. 35, "My grades definitely started . . .": Josh. Personal interview. 1 March 2011.

p. 35, "It wasn't so much about . . .": Josh. Personal interview. 1 March 2011.

CHAPTER 4

pp. 37-38, "I was a monster . . .": Donna. Personal interview.
16 February 2011.

p. 38, "I didn't really have . . .": Donna. Personal interview.
16 February 2011.

p. 38, "The National Survey on Drug Use and Health . .
.": statistical data on the relationship between teenage
drug use and violent behavior, "Youth Violence and
Illicit Drug Use," National Survey on Drug Use and
Health, the Substance Abuse and Mental Health
Services Administration (SAMHSA), 30 December
2008, www.oas.samhsa.gov/2k6/youthViolence/
youthViolence.htm.

p. 39, "short-circuiting": Hanson, Judith. Personal
interview. 1 March 2011.

p. 39, "The teen years are a . . .": Hanson, Judith. Personal
interview. 1 March 2011.

p. 41, "Experts say that almost . . .": statistical data on the
correlation between teen violence and the number of
illicit drugs offenders abuse, "Youth Violence and
Illicit Drug Use," the SAMHSA, 30 December
2008, www.oas.samhsa.gov/2k6/youthViolence/
youthViolence.htm.

p. 42, "When teens begin abusing . . .": Sachs, George.
Personal interview. 27 February 2011.

p. 44, "It was an awful . . .": Gail. Personal interview.
3 October 2011.

p. 44, "We talk and laugh . . .": Gail. Personal interview.
3 October 2011.

NOTES

CHAPTER 5

p. 46, "After I left treatment . . .": Josh. Personal interview. 1 March 2011.

p. 47, "I was at work . . .": Josh. Personal interview. 1 March 2011.

p. 47, "Research indicates that . . .": statistical data on the percentage of people who relapse after receiving treatment for substance abuse, "Understanding Addiction Relapse," Sober Living by the Sea, 19 January 2011, www.soberliving.com/programs/ drug-alcohol-recovery/understanding-addiction- relapse.

p. 48, "I feel like everything's . . .": Josh. Personal interview. 1 March 2011.

p. 53, "After I tried heroin . . .": Tyler. Personal interview. 3 March 2011.

p. 53, "I guess I would . . .": Tyler. Personal interview. 3 March 2011.

p. 55, "Experts estimate that only . . .": statistical data on the percentage of substance abusers that receive treatment, "Treating Adolescents with Addiction," OACBHA, (specific date last updated not available) 2011, www. oacbha.org/wp-content/uploads/2011/Session%20 J%20-%20Treating%20Adolescents%20with%20 Addiction.pdf.

CHAPTER 6

p. 56, "High school is a . . .": Lexie. Personal interview. 2 March 2011.

p. 57, "Research reveals that more . . .": statistical data

on the reported availability of drugs in U.S. schools, "Statistics on Teen Drug Use," Teen Drug Abuse, (specific date last updated not available), www. teendrugabuse.us/teen_drug_use.html.

p. 57, "The most common . . .": Sachs, George. Personal interview. 27 February 2011.

pp. 57-58, "I think more people need . . .": Donna. Personal interview. 2 March 2011.

p. 59, "Adults need to be . . .": Hanson, Judith. Personal interview. 1 March 2011.

p. 60, "According to a recent . . .": statistical data on the percentage of teens who say they would ask their parents for advice about alcohol and drugs, "Parents' Honesty about Own Adolescent Drug Use Inspires Teens Today to Act More Responsibly," *GRAND Magazine*, 8 October 2009, www.grandmagazine.com/ article.asp?id=215.

p. 60, "I went through tough times . . .": Josh. Personal interview. 3 March 2011.

p. 60 and 62, "The wonderful thing about . . .": Josh. Personal interview. 3 March 2011.

Glossary

adolescence the stage of development between childhood and adulthood

comorbid occurring in a patient at about the same time

depressant a drug that reduces activity within a person's nervous system and causes feelings of drowsiness or extreme relaxation

hallucinogen a drug that triggers hallucinations or abnormal physical sensations and mood changes

illicit forbidden or illegal

intravenous describing drugs that are injected into someone's veins

paranoia a mental state that causes a person to be overly sensitive, suspicious, or fearful

paraphernalia equipment or substances used in a certain process or behavior, such as abusing drugs

peers people who share equal standing with others in a larger group

psychotherapy treatment of mental or emotional conditions that typically involves communication with a therapist

relapsed returned to an undesirable behavior such as drug abuse

seizures symptoms of abnormal brain activity that often involve shaking, trembling, or a loss of consciousness

sober unaffected by chemical substances such as drugs and alcohol

stimulant a drug that boosts activity within a person's nervous system and triggers a temporary increase in energy or alertness

traumatized emotionally shocked someone in a way that has long-lasting effects

withdrawal the physical and emotional changes that often occur when a person becomes accustomed to not having a particular drug within his or her body

Further Information

BOOKS

Burlingame, Jeff. *Alcohol.* New York:
Cavendish Square Publishing, LLC, 2014.

Gillard, Arthur (editor). *Marijuana.*
Detroit: Greenhaven Press, 2009.

Marcovitz, Hal. *Drug Abuse.* Detroit:
Lucent Books, 2008.

Wolny, Philip. *Abusing Prescription Drugs.*
New York: Rosen Central/Rosen Publishing,
2008.

WEBSITES

**National Institute on Drug Abuse (NIDA)—
NIDA for Teens**

www.teens.drugabuse.gov

A site that offers games, facts, and real-life
stories related to teen drug abuse.

TeensHealth—Drugs & Alcohol

www.kidshealth.org/teen/drug_alcohol

A website that provides advice on how to seek
help for substance abuse, as well as information
on drugs that are frequently abused by teens.

Bibliography

BOOKS

Bradley, Michael. *When Things Get Crazy with Your Teen: The Why, the How, and What to Do Now.* New York: McGraw-Hill, 2009.

Inciardi, James (editor), and Karen McElrath (editor). *The American Drug Scene: An Anthology.* New York: Oxford University Press, 2008.

Lebow, Jay L. *Handbook of Clinical Family Therapy.* Hoboken, NJ: John Wiley, 2005.

Levinthal, Charles F. *Drugs, Behavior, and Modern Society.* Boston: Allyn & Bacon, 2010.

Winters, Ken C. (editor). *Adolescent Substance Abuse: New Frontiers in Assessment.* New York: The Haworth Press, 2006.

ONLINE ARTICLES

"Drug Abuse and Addiction," *Helpguide,* (specific date last updated not available) November 2010, www.helpguide. org/mental/drug_substance_abuse_addiction_signs_ effects_treatment.htm.

"Drug Treatment for Women," Drug and Alcohol Detoxification Centers, (specific date last updated not available), www.drugalcoholdetoxcenters.com/aarticles-drug-treatment-for-women.html.

"The Essence of Drug Addiction," the National Institutes of Health (NIH), (specific date last updated not available) 2007, www.ncbi.nlm.nih.gov/books/

NBK20368.

"Facts and Figures," the American Foundation for Suicide Prevention (AFSP), (specific date last updated not available) 2011, www.afsp.org/index.cfm?fuseaction= home.viewpage&page_id=050fea9f-b064-4092-b1135c3a70de1fda.

"Fiction: Marijuana Is Harmless," Just Think Twice, (specific date last updated not available), www. justthinktwice.com/factsfiction/fiction_marijuana_is_harmless.html).

"Marijuana and Teens," The San Dieguito Alliance for Drug Free Youth, (specific date last updated not available), www.sandieguitoalliance.org/ marijuanaandteens.html.

"NIDA InfoFacts: Drug Abuse and the Link to HIV/ AIDS and Other Infectious Diseases," the National Institute on Drug Abuse (NIDA), (specific date last updated not available) July 2011, www.nida.nih.gov/ Infofacts/drugabuse.html.

"NIDA InfoFacts: High School and Youth Trends," NIDA, (specific date last updated not available) August 2010, www.drugabuse.gov/infofacts/hsyouthtrends.html.

"Parents' Honesty about Own Adolescent Drug Use Inspires Teens Today to Act More Responsibly," *GRAND Magazine*, 8 October 2009, www.grandmagazine.com/ article.asp?id=215.

"Statistics on Alcohol Abuse," Learn-About-Alcoholism. com, (specific date last updated not available), www. learn-about-alcoholism.com/statistics-on-alcohol-abuse.html.

DRUG ABUSE

"Statistics on Teen Drug Use," Teen Drug Abuse, (specific date last updated not available), www.teendrugabuse. us/teen_drug_use.html.

"Teenage Depression Statistics," Teen Depression, (specific date last updated not available), www.teendepression.org /stats/teenage-depression-statistics.

"Treating Adolescents with Addiction," Ohio Association of County Behavioral Health Authorities (OACBHA), (specific date last updated not available) 2011, www. oacbha.org/wp-content/uploads/2011/Session%20 J%20-%20Treating%20Adolescents%20with%20 Addiction.pdf.

"Understanding Addiction Relapse," Sober Living by the Sea, 19 January 2011, www.soberliving.com/programs/ drug-alcohol-recovery/understanding-addiction- relapse.

"Youth Violence and Illicit Drug Use," Substance Abuse and Mental Health Services Administration (SAMHSA), 30 December 2008, www.oas.samhsa.gov/2k6/youthViolence/ youthViolence.htm.

PERSONAL INTERVIEWS

Donna (February 16, 2011; March 2, 2011; March 3, 2011)
Gail (October 3, 2011)
George Sachs, PsyD (February 27, 2011)
Josh (March 1, 2011; March 3, 2011)
Judith Hanson (March 1, 2011)
Lexie (July 1, 2010; March 2, 2011)
Tyler (March 3, 2011)

Index

Page numbers in **boldface** are illustrations.

About the Author

KATIE MARSICO has authored more than eighty books for children and young adults. She lives in Elmhurst, Illinois, with her husband and children.